Storytelling

Master the Art of Storytelling to Build Trust

(How Storytelling Can Captivate Customers Influence Audiences and Transform Your Business)

Adam Palmer

Published By **Bengion Cosalas**

Adam Palmer

All Rights Reserved

Storytelling: Master the Art of Storytelling to Build Trust (How Storytelling Can Captivate Customers Influence Audiences and Transform Your Business)

ISBN 978-1-7752436-3-2

No part of this guidebook shall be reproduced in any form without permission in writing from the publisher except in the case of brief quotations embodied in critical articles or reviews.

Legal & Disclaimer

The information contained in this book is not designed to replace or take the place of any form of medicine or professional medical advice. The information in this book has been provided for educational & entertainment purposes only.

The information contained in this book has been compiled from sources deemed reliable, and it is accurate to the best of the Author's knowledge; however, the Author cannot guarantee its accuracy and validity and cannot be held liable for any errors or omissions. Changes are periodically made to this book. You must consult your doctor or get professional medical advice before using any of the suggested remedies, techniques, or information in this book.

Upon using the information contained in this book, you agree to hold harmless the Author from and against any damages, costs, and expenses, including any legal fees potentially resulting from the application of any of the information provided by this guide. This disclaimer applies to any damages or injury caused by the use and application, whether directly or indirectly, of any advice or information presented, whether for breach of contract, tort, negligence, personal injury, criminal intent, or under any other cause of action.

You agree to accept all risks of using the information presented inside this book. You need to consult a professional medical practitioner in order to ensure you are both able and healthy enough to participate in this program.

Table Of Contents

Chapter 1: Why Do We Tell Stories? 1

Chapter 2: What is Storytelling and Why is it Important? 25

Chapter 3: Train Your Body................... 57

Chapter 4: Building and Preparing Your Story 71

Chapter 5: Telling Your Story Tips for the Stage... 98

Chapter 6: The facial expressions you display 115

Chapter 7: HYPNOTIC HERO'S JOURNEY 133

Chapter 8: The Ultimate Boon............ 163

Chapter 1: Why Do We Tell Stories?

Before we dive to the heart of what it takes to write and tell an engaging narrative, let's consider the reasons why stories are important to us as humans. What is the source of this almost hypnotic power they wield over us stem from? Why do they have such an impact on us?

The psychology behind Storytelling

Similar to the majority of our habits The concept of storytelling is deeply rooted within our psychological system, which is an outcome of our evolution growth as an animal species. Humans are drawn to patterns. we observe and appreciate causality and effects. It's how we comprehend our surroundings. The premise of the story is simply an example of causality and consequence. A storyteller tells a tale of an incident which led to another which then resulted in another then on and up until reaching an end. It's how life is in the real world which is why we have a huge advantage over the others when we began to appreciate this.

That's why the concept of narrative, or how everything is put into orderly fashion is essential for our lives. We can see it all over our world, and are incredibly excited to discover this. Stories tap into that deep craving for story, fulfilling that desire by offering the viewer an understanding of how the process is in the lives of the individual in the narrative.

If you're in possession of an idea you want to share, there are two options for conveying the message. You might want to convey it your message with a group of individuals who are interested in pursuing your same profession as you have. It's possible to give them the same list with a generic description of all they need to accomplish in order to be successful at what they do and the subjects of study that they'll have to become experts in, the volume of time they'll need to commit, their challenges and so on. It's a generic list that's not too specific to every person. The list could include phrases such as "most successful actors had to live for years taking low-paying bit parts as extras or in commercials" or "if you want to be a successful realtor, you will have to intimately understand how the housing market works".

However it is possible to offer your suggestions in the form of a story, specifically, your tale particularly. A performer could share the story of their own moment of lowly-paid obscurity or a realtor might provide personal tales of her studies in the past, what time and energy it required to complete the course and what obstacles that she encountered. If certain aspects of the journey to the point they're at now didn't be applicable to them and they were unable to fill in the gap with personal stories of coworkers.

The first strategy seems to be very effective - the suggestions would apply to all with no reason for any person to believe it doesn't apply to them specifically. In reality, however, this second method would actually be more efficient. Research has shown that, over a period of time only 5-10% information passed around in the form of simple information remains present and fresh within the brain of the individual who received it, however, an astounding 70%

of the information given as stories remains in the mind of those who receive it. How come this happens?

It's true that the reason for this is because simple information triggers the brain's regions that are able to decode meaning...and that's it. It's not very stimulating in any way. If you listen to a story However, some intriguing things take place within the brain. The brain regions are activated when someone listening was engaged in the activities discussed are triggered. When the storyteller describes something like dancing or walking the motor cortex that controls the movements of our bodies, lights up. When the storyteller talks about an input from the senses, for example the smell of a food item, or a sensation touch The sensory cortex that decodes sensory signals is stimulated. That's on top of the emotional reactions we feel while listening to stories A description of a frightening or tense event triggers fear and anxiety in the background, and resolution of these situations provides an immediate satisfaction. The descriptions of happy and loving circumstances provide us with that warmth and comfort like we're living them.

In the end, the story is more readily and long-lastingly imprints itself on the minds of those who listen to it. The story's details and the emotion it brings to the forefront act as a means of delivering your message or information, transmitting it to the audience and helping to'stick' to the listeners' brains. Another example that shows the potential of stories to permanently imprint themselves on the mind of an audience member is the way they are often a large part of someone's mind that they are able telling the story in the same way as if they were there or even as if the event was actually happening to the person listening to it. Yes, many instances, this happens for an effect that isn't as obvious, or even obvious theft, but the majority of the time this is actually totally unintentional. The tale was well described, and the impressions were so vivid, people who listen to it have completely forgotten that it never actually happened to them.

The impact of a tale doesn't only depend on the kind of details it imparts to the public. The reactions and emotions that it generates are beneficial on their own. Imprinting the emotions of the brain of another like a story can be a powerful and massive thing that helps their brains be in tune with your own. This could be of huge use when trying to influence other people to follow your thoughts by introducing them to your personal patterns of thinking and feelings makes them more open to other thoughts you would like they to embrace. The telling of the tale of an incident or event that has shaped the person you are will impact your readers in exactly the exactly the same way as that event directly affected you.

In the end it is clear that there are four primary goals one can achieve when telling stories. They are not in any particular order. they're - to amuse informing, entertain, guide and to motivate. Every story aims to accomplish one or more of these and are often the most effective and lasting method of doing so. This is power of the light which this book is designed to assist you in capturing and harness for your own benefit in order to change other people's thoughts and create your mark across the globe by telling your story.

The Storyteller's Mindset

After you've gotten an encapsulation of the ways in which stories impact us in the way they do, then you doubt would want to understand how to tap into and use this power efficiently. You may want to skip straight into the next step in which you'll learn about how to stand in front of the camera as well as all the tricks and techniques that can bring people in the palm of your hands However, this could be taking the shot too far an amount.

A excellent story is created even before you step foot on the stage, and in some cases far before you know you'll be a speech which will require you to share a story. Beginning in being a storyteller and changing your mindset to one of.

This chapter takes the look at what is that makes an effective storyteller and will in the process, guide you on the path to becoming a great one.

Many people find it difficult to step on stage to tell an account. One of the main reasons is a fear of the stage itself. Being at the center of attention is among our most fundamental fear, which is fairly normal. In the next section, we will explore ways to conquer this fear further on. However, an part of the reason that people are hesitant to telling stories that's often neglected is that the majority think that they do not have enough tales to share that could inspire or benefit others or that anything that they've ever heard, seen or witnessed could hold the focus of a sceptical audience.

It is simply not true. There are no two lives identical each person has their own collection of life experiences along with a distinctive perspective on the encounters. We've seen that one of the reasons we create stories is because we want to be a part our lives with others and be able to see how other people think and feel. So even the most common or mundane experiences in your own life can be a source of inspiration. Strange things occur in and around us all often And the reality is that most people do not even notice these events.

The first step in becoming a successful storytelling artist is to get over the notion that you aren't a good storyteller. any interesting stories to share with the world. If you truly embrace the idea that your life could be the source of inspiring and interesting stories, you'll see incredible new perspectives that open their doors for the world.

In order to put this philosophy into application, you must be alert and engaged in any interaction that you engage in. The qualities that distinguish good storytellers from the rest of us - is that person within your group of buddies who has never any shortage of stories to tell, or the globally well-known speaker who is regularly to audiences at least a thousand - is that they are always looking to every meeting they attend and scrutinize every aspect of their lives to find interesting stories. It is also important to adopt the same mindset. If you search for intriguing moments within your daily life You will see them.

If you apply the tips that is later in the guide, you'll be able to create an idea or a lesson that you wish to impart while telling an account. These lessons are known to have the habit of appearing that you would least think of them and only becoming evident as you think about them in the future. A situation may appear to be completely unrelated and insignificant when it's occurring to you, however it is possible that it may prove valuable to show something that you didn't think you could have.

This method can also be used for creating a story of your entire life spans many years. Many times, you might be asked to share the story of things that took place in a lengthy period of time. This could include a recounting of your work experience, telling of your efforts to win over your spouse or the time of struggle you had to endure in a number of instances. The narratives are made from individual incidents which means that you'll not have the ability to build the story and present the story convincingly without these seemingly small specifics. Much like the learnings are derived from past events may only become apparent in the past however, the larger picture will often be hidden from the person immersed in the story. Pay attention to everything around you regardless of whether it appears relevant at the time or not.

Naturally, you aren't the sole protagonist of your tales, it's unlikely that you'll only want to tell or tell stories about you. It is possible to choose asked to share a story about someone else from your life. It could be a story where you won't have even been involved. For this to be successful, you'll need to show more than a superficial interest in the individuals who surround you. In addition to paying attentively to events that occur within your lives, you should develop a keen curiosity about the events that occur within the lives of other people. Keep an eye on how you are with them, so you be aware of their character and enjoy their story. So, you'll have the ability to construct an accurate and well-rounded portrayal of their character and add yet another source of content to your library.

Another kind of story that you could be required to share are stories that you have written including popular tales, legends and folktales. Being able to demonstrate an interest in these stories and an understanding of them will aid you greatly. If you're constantly in the process of reading or listening to others tell stories then you'll first of be able to have a greater knowledge of how they are put together and also of the best way to communicate them. In addition, you can also prepare a few of them available whenever you're asked to address a group.

Most of the time, creating the fictional stories of your dreams is a matter for the written word, however there are instances where it is suitable, or if you're explicitly asked to do the same thing. A few examples of scenarios it is appropriate are discussing an event in which you don't have any directly or indirectly experienced of and also if you're discussing a subject that is extremely sensitive that you'd like to keep identities private or preserve the privacy of those who've been through it or you want to convey an argument that isn't exactly hit the nail in the face with something which you've actually experienced.

Each of the suggestions above are vital in order to craft impressive, authentic and enjoyable fiction. Any good story however fantastical it may be, has origins in the real world and our everyday human interactions that we have in common. Be aware of things happening around you can give you plenty of ideas and will give you a solid basis to build your story. The characters you create need be convincing to allow your readers to be able to relate with them which means you'll require greater than a basic knowledge of the way other people perceive and act. The act of listening and reading storylines will provide you with an understanding of the way they're constructed, and what you can do to best convey the stories.

Naturally, it can be a challenge to keep an accurate record of all your events and to be able find it at any time and at a high level, which is why you'll likely have to write down your experience in a form that's not as prone to error as the memory of your brain. One option is to maintain a diary that you keep track of events that occur to you everyday that interest you or that have a significant moral or personal value. It's not necessary to get in to the smallest detail. A basic outline of what aspects of your experience that stand in your mind most will provide enough information to jog the memory of you when looking over your journal at a later date. Every now and then, review your journals and go over what you've written in the earlier years. It serves two purposes as it lets you examine the incidents through the lens of hindsight, and when their role in the timeline of your life has become more clear, and it helps refresh your memories to help you better recall the events while you're writing the story you want to tell.

In the same way, it is important to keep a record of the stories you've heard from others around you about their personal experiences, in your journals along with different kinds of stories you read or hear in order to more easily recall them if you're required to.

In addition to this the best storytellers realize that they will never master enough of the art of storytelling. However advanced you are in the field of storytelling There will always be an opportunity to improve. There's always more to learn and a new strategy you can use to make your tales even more interesting and full.

Keep this in mind and constantly look out for opportunities that will help you expand your capabilities. There are many books on how to create better stories, and also improving your performance and performance on stage. Be on the lookout for these books which can assist you in becoming more proficient at telling stories. There are also classes on the art of telling stories and public speaking. If you're a student at an institution of higher learning nearby you, chances are they have open courses that you could take part in. Even those who don't most likely have the top way to find information to you. Internet is an excellent source - there are classes and tutorials on a variety of various websites that focus on ongoing education as well in streaming sites such as Youtube.

A skilled storyteller is aware that it's impossible to master the art in isolation. The lessons, as well as the psychological reinforcement of ideals for storytelling around the world will never be enough. You must watch others do it in order to receiving feedback on your method.

Take a look at others storytellers do their thing in live performance or on video. Begin to befriend and socialize with other storytellers, and make use of their experiences to share ideas and take lessons from them. Especially the ones who have more experience in their craft than you are and whom you can aspire to be like. This isn't to suggest that it isn't a good idea to take time to spend time with people who aren't yet at their level of proficiency, but watching them make mistakes could aid in identifying some of the ones you have made, while also teaching other storytellers is one of the most efficient methods to learn.

Small-scale, regional storytelling festivals are beginning to grow in terms of attention in large cities today. They are an excellent opportunity to meet like-minded individuals as well as a chance to develop your skills as a storyteller. These events are generally more laid-back and carry a lower risk as opposed to events where you are in front of a huge audience or pressure to do it all at once. This means that there is a more relaxed atmosphere in which to experiment with new ideas and make mistakes until you succeed and not worry about missing a crucial opportunity to communicate your message.

Making your mind more positive is never-ending. It is essential to be vigilant about your mind, ensuring that you look at every experience by considering the way you can transform it into a compelling story. taking advantage of every chance to improve your skills by observing and learning from the experiences of others. If you stay true to this, you'll be able to develop and become more effective and compelling writer.

Ability to create the tale ... this could be the most potent skills one has. This isn't just about telling every story. We're talking about the ability to transform an everyday story and change into something appealing, captivating and leave the reader being in the top position of the world or laughing out loud... perhaps perhaps making them cry, near crying.

It could be a neighbour, someone you have met at a local café or perhaps an auditorium filled with people eager to be inspired ... It could be children perhaps, or even your children while you put them to bed to get a restful night's sleep.

The fact that you are naturally a storyteller is fantastic since it implies that they already have the abilities required to create a compelling story. But the best part is that everyone can, including you, is able to learn to be a great storyteller. All you require is appropriate tools and techniques (which we're offering you right in the present) as well as the desire to put your hand into the game and increase your proficiency in telling stories.

Stories are a great tool to use across the globe. They're a way to disseminate new ideas as well as the foundation for new partnerships.

Chapter 2: What is Storytelling and Why is it Important?

In this part in this section, we'll give an overview of storytelling, and explain what it's used for before diving into ways to create a compelling story that is compelling, memorable, and powerful.

The art of telling stories is one which has existed since the dawn of time. The term "storytelling" can be described as an ancient form of art that allows individuals to express their ideas and opinions in an engaging manner that sparks the mind of the audience.

The art of storytelling is a two-way avenue. The storyteller is there, after which you will have the audience. The way that the listener reacts to the storyteller usually decides the next step of the storyteller dependent on the kind of response they're searching to get.

Let's consider a comedian who is good to give an example. The comedians pay attention to the reactions from the audience to decide which direction they will take the in the next. Do they want to see more laughter? Do you want people to be stunned? Would he like an emotional reaction? Would he like the audience to be awed? What kind of reaction seeks is his ability to achieve it through taking notes and observing the effect his story has on the people before him.

Storytellers employ the spoken and body languages to communicate the story's events and characters the story usually through voice as well as physical movements.

The Social Experience

Stories have always been a great method of entertainment. It is a great event for adults as well as youngsters. The audience can get caught with a tale that before they know you know it, someone is in a state of laughter, or could have an angry look on their faces, depending upon the style of tale you're sharing. Stories are capable to invoke emotional responses. They can be a great way to instantly establish a connection with a person.

Having an Attractive Personality

A beautiful persona is essential. If you have dull personality... Sorry I'm sorry, but you won't achieve much with this persona. If you are speaking in public, it's important to talk clearly and focus on the words you speak. If you are seated and talk as if you were reading an outline, the audience is losing interest and will and get up from their seats, and go away and never return.

I'd like to ask you one question: What is the factor that causes people to attract them? What's the secret behind their magnetic character? The ability to entertain and an insane amount of it... Any person looking to become an effective storyteller should take the time to study the art of telling stories and learn how to master the craft. Learning to master anything, including an incredible charisma requires 10,000 hours, according to the experts. So, you need to start now!

A Great Drive to Succeed:

The people with deep determination are likely to appreciate their time too excessively to spend their time on activities which are not worth it. The majority of people choose those who have an attitude of direction and purpose... the ones who are driven tend to be the most likely to make an impact.

Communicate Considerately:

Speak sincerely. Listen lovingly. Stay present to others and demonstrate your appreciation.

Look for the Best in Others:

You must be searching to be the best in others since if you do not, you'll appear fake. It's possible to "fake it till you make it" however it's difficult to create a fake image with no one noticing. Do you really wish to look untrue? If you're not authentic, you will lose your credibility and your life lost if cannot keep it under control. Finding the top to others is crucial.

Enthusiasm:

The most significant thing since it's probably the most visible aspect of who we are, aside from being an introvert and extrovert. The expression of enthusiasm shows the passion you have for your own self and, if you're projecting your enthusiasm towards others, then they're showing enthusiasm as well. The importance of enthusiasm is that it's not a good idea to be that dull man at the end of the table.

Humor is a Good Thing:

If you're looking to go with the approach of telling stories with humor the use of humor is the most important thing. If you are planning to become an entertaining storyteller, then you might as well not have the privilege of being an actor. The ability to laugh relieves stress as it changes from the stressful issue to the fresh one that has a great beginning in the beginning. The key is engaging other people as you make others amused.

Calm and Composed:

Perhaps you have noticed people with beautiful personalities tend to be serene and peaceful. This is a sign of a healthy self-esteem. In addition, this kind of mental attitude can put other people to ease immediately.

Just Smile:

People judge someone's behavior without actually knowing the amount of smiles they show. Smiles show how much you truly care about aspects of your life. It reveals your heart and your personality. It reveals the person that is easy to reach that is a major benefit for anyone. There is also an engagement aspect since smiles can be infectious.

Don't Worry:

A lot of people don't succeed their storytelling skills because they worry about what people are thinking about themselves. Don't worry about what other people consider you to be and live your life and live your life as you are. Think about what people would like to imagine about your character, and don't stress about making an impression. As I mentioned before Be yourself. When you show your true self people will appreciate your authenticity.

The process of implementing these important points isn't something that can be done in a day as it takes years and years of practice to get them right, however starting earlier is always a great idea. What's more, you can do them all and start now!

Get Excited

An effective storyteller is engaging their audience in an unforgettable journey that will leave people feeling encouraged and enthused. Sure, structuring your talk to allow you to get your message through to the audience in order to keep their attention could be difficult also.

If you are starting out how do you begin? Are you starting by presenting the information you'd prefer to communicate? It's not the best route to go down. Human brains are wired to tell tales - they are drawn to adventures and heroes, as well as layers, unexpected events, and most importantly happy endings.

Presenting before crowds of people even though it's only just three or less people is a source of anxiety and anxiety. While you prepare to present your talk it is possible that you have many concerns running through your brain and include whether or not people are going to like the presentation you plan to say, whether the voice is shaking or if you're prepared, and the range of possible questions are endless. If you're worried you're thinking toward negative thoughts when your event approaches, you'll are feeling more stressed than you have ever. This can result in issues that occur when you present, and this can cause you to believe that the worst was destined to happen.

Are you interested in knowing my secret for how to deliver a thrilling speech? The trick is to get enthusiastic about the topic! Let's take a basketballer as an example, making preparations to represent his country the first time in a world stage. He's done many hours in training. He's been through the entire drills and is well-prepared to deal with any situation which may happen. Before he goes into the match there is no fear of things taking off in a negative direction. He is simply brimming with energy and enthusiasm flowing throughout his body as he is looking forward to revealing his most impressive moves and delight his audience who are looking at him.

Prior to presenting your talk Begin your presentation by having positive thoughts that you repeat in your head. This could be "the audience will love me" or "this is going to be fun." When you turn towards positive affirmations, you are able to relax with the comfort knowing this puts your in the best state of mind and you'll be comfortable enough to perform before an crowd, no matter what size or number they could be.

Here are a few tips to make you more excited about the next event in your storytelling calendar...

Get Prepared. If you are really keen to become engaged in storytelling You must be ready. This means spending the time necessary to work on your presentation until you're sure that you've got it right. The best practice is to do an evening of rehearsals or on a regular basis - it will provide you with sense of security when facing that crowd. If you're in the process of making your plans, speak the tale in front of the audience so you hear yourself clearly and observe what you sound like. While you're practicing be aware of the tone you use. Perform this exercise on your own after which, once you're prepared then have a buddy or loved ones listen to your. If you're interested in knowing how you appear as you tell the story, utilize a video camera.

Create something new - as you prepare to share your tale, your main goal is to hook your viewers. The first thing to focus on is how you'll tell the story. There are a variety of methods you may choose to use, depending on the end result you'd like to attain. Choose from the following methods: Spark Lines and The Mountain... I will discuss the two techniques at the conclusion in this section.

The story should end in a positive way Your conclusion to your tale should be strong and powerful. The ending should be strong enough that it's able to draw your audience's attention to. In order to do this, you must highlight some of the most important aspects you discussed at the beginning of your presentation and help to demonstrate the way your presentation came all the way around. If the audience departs the room, they must leave with the expectation of making their next decision.

If you want to get enthusiastic, you'll have to be able to think out of the space when you tell your story. It is essential to think of different ways of using visual aids. You might want to think about what you'll wear for a more authentic tale. In the event of preparing your presentation, you should have an end goal in mind. it is determined by your expectations to get from your audience. final goal.

Let's take a look at the various storytelling models I've talked to you about in the past...

The Mountain:

The structure helps to define the tension and drama while telling the story. The Mountain does not necessarily come to an ending that's pleasant. The first chapter you'll set the stage, and this will then be later followed by smaller challenges. Then, you'll increase in action just before the ultimate final.

Imagine this like a TV show. Every episode is going to have many challenges and ups leading up to the final episode which occurs near the conclusion of the season.

The Mountain is Good For:

* Gradually increasing tension with the audience

Then, you can show your public how to conquer challenges in a series of obstacles

- Providing a conclusion which will satisfy

Sparklines:

It is an approach to create a map of presentation structure. A great deal of speech success since they are able to take the ordinary world and transform it into the idealized, better world. It basically compares the present with what might be. Do you think that makes sense?

Sparklines stimulates the desire to changes in the crowd. It's an emotionally-driven technique which will inspire the crowd to follow your lead.

Sparklines are Good For:

* Inspiring excitement

• Inspiring the crowd

Petal Structure:

This structure is one that is used when you had to group several stories or presentations around a common theme.

If you've got a variety of unrelated tales you'd like to share, or something you'd like be able to reveal it is this structure you'd be using.

The process involves telling your tales in order, and then returning to your principal tale. It is possible to overlap the petals in the way that one story opens an idea to the next one, however each story is supposed to be a full story.

This type of storytelling can let your viewers know how the stories in these important tales are connected to one another. They will be able to feel the importance of the tale.

The Petal is Great for:

* Showing how various scenarios relate to one main idea.

• Explaining how the strands of the story connect.

The truth is that storytelling can be an art form - it's something that you are able to make or break, according to what "picture" you choose to create. It's possible to create an exciting experience and truly captivate the audience. Or, you could make it dull and lead your audience to the exit. What you choose to do is yours to choose - which among these methods of telling are you going to employ?

Getting Over Your Fear of Speaking In Public

We'll begin by calling your fear by its term - some call it "stage fright," while others prefer the more technical name "glossophobia."

Glossophobia is sometimes referred to as anxiety of speech. It originates in the Greek words glossa (tongue) and the Greek word phobos (dread or fear). This is an extreme anxiety about public speaking or even speaking at all. This is among the most commonly-experienced fears across our world at present. The majority of people in the population suffers from it, however with different degrees. It has been reported by more than people who suffer from claustrophobia (the anxiety of being enclosed) as well as agoraphobia (the fear of heights) as well as Arachnophobia (the anxiety of spiders).

A few signs of glossophonbia are the following symptoms:

* Remaining frozen with your target audience

* Dry mouth

* Nausea

* Dizziness

* Hands numbing

* Breathing shortness

* Shaking

* Panic attacks

* Sweating

* Shaky Voice

Some experts have said that dread experienced by some pupils about being asked by their instructor to stand in front of their class or even to respond to the teacher's question is a prime sign of glossophobia.

Then, what is it that causes shyness of speaking to the public? There are many factors that could be blamed on the reason for one's anxiety about speaking in public...

The environment or the upbringing of one's child while Growing up who grew up in a setting that did make it difficult to develop confidence and courage in dealing with crowds and even having conversations with a lot of people, tend to feel unconfident and lower self-esteem. In turn, they is a reason why they avoid speaking in the public.

Traumatic experiences - There are occasions when an individual might be a victim of an incident in which they were speaking publicly which resulted in the most embarrassing time. The people who had this kind of encounter are more likely to avoid the possibility of being in similar situations again since they are afraid that the embarrassing incident could happen again.

A Lack of familiarity with the concept of speaking in public - The human mind can be scared of the things that they're not comfortable with. Therefore, persons who aren't exposed to public speaking are likely to be reluctant whenever it's time to take the stage in the spotlight.

Speech Problems There are people who suffer from speech issues including speech stuttering. These people tend to avoid speaking out in public.

Treatment to Help Get Over the Fear of Public Speaking:

Therapy: A Cognitive-Behavioral therapy is a popular treatment option for people who want to overcome their fear of speaking publicly. With cognitive-behavioral therapy patients will have the chance to discover ways to counter those messages of fear they are receiving with positive self-talk and positive thinking. This type of therapy can be particularly beneficial in those who have anxiety when faced with the prospect of standing to speak in public. By using this method of treatment one will be taught the most effective techniques for relaxation which they can employ to manage these anxiety attacks. When they can manage these types of attacks, they'll be able to manage them better.

Virtual Reality Therapy - Some claim that VR therapy also works to aid those suffering from social anxiety. In this kind of therapy, the patient is placed in a virtual space which simulates public speaking. They will then be required to give their speech repeatedly, just to simulate reality.

Medicines - There are real medications to which people may have been prescribed by them. They may help in calming anxiety or nervousness of the patient. In reality most of the time they are intended to be taken when patients are undergoing cognitive-behavioral treatment, not used on their own. There are many beta-blockers individuals who use them to ease the pain of extreme fear or nerves. Beta-blockers can help reduce anxiety due to their characteristics which block adrenaline's action. Patients should take caution of this, however, since there are a variety of adverse effects that could be experienced when using these medications. That's that this treatment is handled with a degree of caution.

Self-Help is a method that typically is available when the patient has dealt with their fears. The focus of these methods is making sure that the control the patient holds over their fears of speaking publicly will last forever. Also, medication as well as therapy can help individuals overcome the fear of speaking in public and self-help methods can help them feel more confident giving a speech before the crowd or an audience.

Choosing the Best Treatment Option:

There is a vast selection of treatment options for patients to choose from however, not all are suitable for everyone. When deciding which option to take, it's crucial to take into consideration the following:

The reason for the Fear The root of this fear in the first place? Perhaps it's due to the traumatizing event which occurred within the past and can be difficult to overcome? Are you suffering from an issue with stuttering? Perhaps you are just afraid of talking in public?

If you want to determine what you should say it is first necessary to determine what the root of the irrational fear you have to speak in public.

The real nature of Fear The real reason you are afraid is what are you scared of? Perhaps it is that you might confuse your fear of performance in general with the fear of speaking to a crowd? Certain people feel comfortable speaking in front of groups of people. However when they are required to do something different then they stop. As an example, certain actors feel comfortable performing lines on stage. However, when interviewing, they slow down.

Understanding what it is you're fearful of makes it simpler to identify what kind of care that you require to overcome the fear you have of speaking out in public.

It is the Severity of the Issue - The issue is the severity of fear. The solution could be found through various sessions of consoling. In addition there are other causes that require both medication as well as cognitive-behavioral therapy are required.

Let me share a few facts with You - Are you familiar with the pro golfer Tiger Woods? He was born with speech difficulties. Unbelievable, right? Yes, when you examine him today you'll be unable to tell that the fact is that he was a child who stutters that made him fearful of speaking in public. If you asked him how he came over this fear, he explained that he concentrated on correcting the issue with his speech. He practiced for a long time, talking to his dog. He always maintained a positive outlook on matters. He always pictured himself as positive to stay in the right direction. If you think about it, that you can learn by the way he conquered the fear that he had. First finding the source of the issue, and then focused on resolving it prior to went on to the next step. After he uncovered the source of the issue He was determined and did not give up until he achieved the results he wanted.

Be patient and take Your Time - I understand that you'd like to begin talking to the public immediately ... perhaps you're not ready to do it at the moment, but you're trying to conquer the fear of speaking in public so you're able to enjoy telling stories. It's crucial that you do not rush the process.

Don't rush through the story Also, on the other hand It is crucial that you do not hurry through the tale. Sure, you'll want to complete the task and get it completed as swiftly as you can, and so you might feel the need to speed through the tale. But, rapid-talking has an ability to make it hard to breathe.

Three key steps you need to take if you are afraid when speaking in front of the public and telling your tale:

Do not show your fear - Keep your face unfocused (or calm). Additionally, manage any tremors you might feel with your hands or legs.

Sit Still - If your anxious, even when performing, it's an indication that you're stressed.

Be careful not to speak too fast. If you speak fast it's likely that you'll get stuttery, which will only exacerbate the issue. Be careful with your words and pronounce them correctly. Are you talking in a slow pace? If you speak too slow, others around you will be in a position to understand your words.

Further Tips on Getting Over the Fear of Speaking in Public:

Learn to Train Classes and classes you could attend. The classes you attend are connected to public speaking. They can prove beneficial for those looking to overcome the fear of glossophobia. The classes can help you conquer this fear. However, they also will teach you to become more comfortable making public appearances.

Join Support Groups and be more proactive - Have you already been a member of support groups? This is a great first step, but don't end there. Make sure to expand your network of friends through taking the initiative to join other groups, and taking part in activities that can bring you in contact with greater numbers of individuals. A drama class, for instance is a good move.

In no time you'll feel comfortable with the concept of being able to communicate with three or more individuals at once.

Join Organizations - There's many groups you could join that will help reinforce what you've learnt up to this point. It will help you get started with practicing your speaking skills in small groups, till you're ready to make towards speaking to the larger crowd.

Get Your Mind Working Make sure you take at least 5 minutes every day for yourself, and then try to take a break by allowing your mind to get a workout. Relax in a calm location with your spine straight. supported with the back of your comfortable chair. Relax your eyes and breathe. Control your breathing until you sense the air moving into out. As your mind starts to wander, concentrate on your breathing. The breathing will help you return to your center of attention.

It's true that practice makes perfect. the truth, you can practice to become perfect! Like Tiger Woods did, you have to work hard and not quit.

Whatever you believe it's today, in the end, it will become easier. Beginning by telling tales that you are passionate about and are knowledgeable about.

Chapter 3: Train Your Body

If you are able to use your body's ability to share stories, it's just like your heart in the telling of the tale, making it more captivating. Think about it this way: what would you prefer to watch, someone who sits in a sterile place not moving a limb, and talks about a story or someone who makes use of their body in order to communicate the tale? Personally, I am annoyed when someone just stands on the ground and tells stories and does not show any kind of emotion... it simply isn't flowing well.

Your voice as well as your body are both powerful tools that you can utilize to boost your the communication... Fortunately they are simple to learn. They are able to be trained, similar to muscles for support in the storytelling. In this section of my book I'm going to show how you can work with your

Using Gestures in Public Speaking:

Let's begin with a discussion of gestures. Gestures, if you follow a basic principle, could aid in understanding your point. It's important to avoid using gestures that are not in line with what you're trying to convey, since these are not good.

Be sure to prepare your gestures prior to when the story is told. Make a list of the requirements of the gesture, not of just the gesture in the gesture itself. In a matter of minutes in the right moment the appropriate move will occur. The viewers will be able to see something natural and more than likely support your message.

Do not forget to breathe at least twice repeatedly... It is crucial that you realize your most significant goal is to be at ease - it will make it much easier to relate your story. When you're at the safety of your home and are comfortable, you'll be able to use your mind creativity, planning, and creativity more easily before you even breathe.

Begin by starting from a neutral starting from the neutral position. It means that you need to be seated with your hands by the side of your body, bringing your hands upwards to create the gesture. If you are making the gesture, ensure you make it clear and precise. Do not ever repeat the motion, or even a halfway one. Once you've made your move and then return your hands back to your "neutral" position.

What is the purpose of gesturing? Actually, using gestures will help you achieve various tasks. Gestures support your words in addition to telling people that you're at ease, since the hands aren't on top of each other.

Descriptive Gestures:

Descriptive gestures are the gestures you could use to convey an event or tell a story. They are very significant in the eyes of those around your face because it demonstrates enthusiasm. There is no one sitting there in front of their the side.

Of course, the most common form of expressive gestures is to use your hands. This can be done by making random hand-waving gestures to show your interaction to viewers or utilize them to describe. When you're discussing something massive and you want to convey the magnitude, simply extend your arms in a wide way. While we're discussing this scenario you can illustrate contrasts, such as conveying something very small and an extremely large thing. This can show the thing you're trying to convey and draw attention of people.

It is also possible to use them to display numbers, quantities or objects, and so on. They are very useful when telling a story but you won't be able to create a compelling story the use of words alone. Through descriptive gestures, you can build a more profound impression of the story we are telling and enhance the engagement of the audience.

Emotional Gestures:

Be aware of the use of emphatic gestures. They are often known as emotional gestures. If, for instance, you're depressed, you try to play your own to yourself (physically) and then tell the sad portion of the tale. If you're angry portion of the story you could pretend to kick into the air and then put your angry expression on. You should employ these gestures in order to convey your feelings throughout the tale. The use of strong gestures can make you seem more authentic when you tell the tale.

Do not Force it. Simply put, if you force something to happen, you appear to be fake unless you're a professional fraudster. Falsehood is not the best thing for anyone as stated previously and all you'll accomplish will be hurting you in the long term. The key is practicing and preparing before telling your story. Allow the movements to speak for themselves Don't allow your brain dictate your movements, let your mouth be the sole control.

Avoid actions that do not add worth or don't contribute to the story you're telling. They can derail the presentation by sending two distinct messages that be a sign that you do not understand what you're talking about or you're trying to force your audience to believe that you're presenting it in a way that's not true. Simply let it out in a natural way.

Some of the worst gestures I have seen include doing hair-styles It's a bad one for women since hair just sits there, ready to be used. Making adjustments to your clothes is another bad gesture. This could be a necessary move in a majority of cases however, avoid it for the majority times since it could show a lack of effort.

Your Physical Expression:

If you're sharing your story to the your public setting, be mindful of the art of expression. Your expression on your face throughout the tale could be the difference between success or failure of the whole experience. If you're at a joyful portion of the story, you should have a smile If you're in an unsatisfactory part of the story, then there shouldn't be a smiling face. You should ensure that your expressions shift when you're telling your story. Take the fascinating facts you'll need to convey to your audience and discover the expression that is appropriate to the tale.

The Power of the Pause:

If you're telling a story, especially when you're just beginning to learn about telling stories, stopping is one of the most difficult things you'll ever attempt for on your first try. When you're talking to people, they are prone to pause just because they're not sure the topic they'd like to speak about. However, since you're prepared for a talk, it is much easier to let a pause happen with your enthusiasm trying to break out.

As humans, we are conditioned to give value to every minute and, for an essay, the words. We believe that we must to ensure that our writings are longer than we can, however, it's rarely as long by the caliber of the essay.

Also, we will increase the anticipation for what's to come as what's the use of creating such an elaborate story in the first place if there's no value? Expectation leads to retention and that's exactly what you need from the story.

I'll show you how to make the most of the potential of the Pause...

The first step is to start with a the silence. It takes a lot of courage at times to stand in front of a crowd that you've never seen before when you've been introduced to the stage, and not speak something right away. However, it is the most effective approach to gaining that attention that you want. This creates an environment of questioning where people are paying attention as they're eager to get the answers. This also causes tension because of the doubt the brain generates automatically.

If you're the one to share your story begin by sitting there in silence while you look at people in the crowd, and let people make eye contact to them. When you're sure everyone's relaxed and eagerly awaiting the tale with excitement Start with a lively tale.

You'll be sure be amazed at the level of interest it draws. Because you've created an intimacy through silence, people will be ready for you to announce the big announcement. Just ensure that you do not screw the whole thing up because it's dangerous if you fail.

Stop with a Purpose:

In the course of telling a story, there's a point that pauses are necessary to add significance and allow the audience the chance to enjoy, take in or adapt to what you stated. After you've made your story's main points and you are done, stop the conversation for 5 minutes. It helps us absorb the information and note them down. It's true that we should take an interruption from what other people have to say, but we should also absorb it and keep a record of it. If somebody claims they do, then they're in fact lying.

Intervals and Transitions

While telling that tale and you're jumping between parts of the story to another without warning the audience will be left in confusion with a look of dismay at their faces. It's because there was no pause or let them keep up with the narrative you're telling. In the event that this occurs, the listeners will tend to take a break from the story even though they appear to be staring at them. In addition, if you pause your speech correctly, your listeners are given the chance to get ready for the next section of the story.

Twitching:

A majority of people exhibit an anxious twitch, which is evident when doing some activity which can give stress. The nervous movements can affect the effectiveness of your presentation and can include tapping the feet, shifting the weight from one side to another, or moving in a random manner. To determine what's happening when you share your story, observe yourself as you record and listen to the replay. In this way, you can be able to see what part of your speech you must enhance to make it better.

Drink Water:

A minimum of ten minutes prior to when you are scheduled to stand before your audience, drink a glass of water. If you're stressed in any way it's likely that you'll be left with dry mouth. Your voice's clarity could be affected because you're not able to produce sufficient saliva for swallowing. The water can help keep the tongue from getting stuck against the mouth's roof while you're telling the narrative.

Get your style on:

Did you watch any presenters? Some are prone moving between the stages such that your neck and eyes could become exhausted trying to keep up. You can also find the ones who're so unmoving and rigid that their voices sound monotone. If you're trying to convey the story of your life in a compelling manner, then you'll need to add some movement to your presentation. Let yourself walk slowly across the stage. You can stop your movements when you need to make a aspect. Be aware that it's not like walking up and down the stage. This is simply the sign that you are nervous. At times you should move toward the crowd, as they will notice you more.

At the end of the day, when you tell that tale, you must perform it with grace. When you're on the stage, do it effortlessly and elegantly Be the persona that you were created to be, and you won't struggle to get your audience.

Chapter 4: Building and Preparing Your Story

When you've completed the continuous practice of refining your thinking however, there's much more work to be completed before you are able to get your message out there on the stage. The next set of steps starts once you've received confirmation that the event is happening - that you've been contacted or selected as a speaker. You you know the date along with the location, composition of the audience, the subject matter and more. This is when you start preparing for the particular event, preparing the story you want to tell and prepping your thoughts for the event.

The stage of preparation for this is crucial - this is the place where you create and refine your story. The lack of preparation shows in many negative effects on stage. The story you tell will not flow, it will lack emotional power and fails to provide meaningful information. The same problem can be seen on your physical and mental side in that you aren't aware of the story from beginning to end results in nervousness, as well as all troubles and tics that come to this.

The next chapter will give you a step-by-step procedure for creating an engaging story that doesn't be able to flow just like water out of your head, but also get into the heads of people watching in a manner which will entice their attention and leave them inspired and content.

Step 1: Determine your goal

We looked at the goals of telling stories in the very first chapter. Deciding what your goals for telling the story to be the primary thing you consider when planning the day of the telling. The goal will determine every step you take starting from choosing the specific experience you'll draw inspiration from until the way you present yourself when you are on stage.

In the first place, regardless of regardless of any other rules that you might be required to adhere to, you'll want to keep your viewers' attention. This is why having fun isn't just an option, it's essential. It's not just about making your audience squeal in laughter, or shouting and gasping excitedly, but. The most entertaining stories are those that captivates your audience's feelings which covers the whole spectrum from excitement and joy to the emotion of pathos (the emotion of pity as well as sadness) as well as hope, affection, and encouraging. It is the emotion that brings us together and is the primary theme in your stories.

The details of your event determines which additional goals you'll take on your own to accomplish. In some cases, it is enough to just entertain people which is a particular case in informal or friendly settings. If you're sharing stories with your friends at a fire pit or in bars, absolutely make your tale as simple and enjoyable as you can. A majority of scheduled events in which you're invited to share your story are likely to require extra from you. What they want from you is typically not only to be entertaining but rather to leave the crowd with the knowledge that they have acquired something that they did not have prior to and most likely would not otherwise.

Step 2: Add an idea of a moral or message to your story, and then connect the story to your personal experience

This is a step that's intricately linked to the first and has the same purpose to give your story the an edge and giving your readers an understanding from your story. The distinction is that the goal is yours solely, while your content is clearly stated. This will allow viewers to feel connected with the story.

To ensure that your message is remembered it is important to connect the message to your own experiences. It is important to create directly between them to strengthen one another. There are two ways from that you could look at the connection between your messages and your experience. In some instances, you may be presented with an exact message that you're trying to deliver either through a written or oral message, or determined by the context of the occasion, specifically, the person you're communicating to. If this is the case, choose a tale from your savings account that will convey the intended content.

For instance for an example, if you are preparing the speech to accept any award, it is possible to convey that the hard work you put into it brought you there, and paying tribute to those who supported you in the course of your journey. Based on that the idea, you could then select an example that illustrates the points above - for instance, reminiscing about an undertaking you completed along with your colleagues which brought the group praise and even success.

There are occasions when you may be asked to give a speech at events that do not have a subject, or perhaps one in which the participants are encouraged to create the story of your own. It is possible to choose a theme prior to choosing the story that best illustrates the message, however another option is to do it the opposite direction - choose an idea that you believe will be intriguing to your public and enjoyable to share and then study the story to determine what lesson you could incorporate into the story.

The message you send will help to decide which parts of the story you want to highlight to focus your attention particularly on the ones that support your claim. What you need to think about of what elements of the story you should place special emphasis on will need to be considered during the following step.

STEP 3: Put together the content you want to include

After you have used your goal and purpose to choose the tale you wish to tell, you'll be able to tweak your story's contents to make it more effective. In the beginning, ensure that you write everything down precisely how you recall the details. If you've got it written in a journal, this should be a breeze - simply writing it down and adding the details you might not have recorded. In the moment the story you've written is very raw. It's likely interesting all on it's own way, but it's best to tweak the story so that it is interesting and engaging and also to be certain that the story conveys the message clearly and will appeal to the specific demographic of your target audience.

Three elements to play with during this process - the setting along with the character and specifics. Let's look at each separately each in turn.

The Situation

Then we'll get into some important, hard to digest parts: how can you structure the setting of your story in a way that will engage and entice your audience? In the first place, you must tailor the story for your target audience. The story should be one which they can relate to or something that they've been through or have experienced or they might hope for or anticipate to occur to them. If the audience isn't able to connect to the story in a certain way, then there is no chances of retaining their attention.

If you are addressing a particular issue or talking to a particular sort of crowd, the work is typically done for you. If, for instance, you're invited to address at an event for students on a Careers Day, you highlight the subject matter that is connected with your academics along with the educational and professional course you chose to follow. If you're given the subject, you select the elements of the narrative that you can relate to and highlight them.

If you're speaking to a larger kind of audience however, there are several ways to adapt your message to their needs. There are common themes of the human experience that everyone can recognize - being in love, discovering the path you want to take, or overcoming any obstacle, there are a myriad of possibilities. The inspiration for your story comes from these. is usually a good option, however if you are looking to make a statement, it is possible to focus your story on an aspect that is individual and specific to your needs. It is also a good idea to read stories in order to get different perspectives. So you could discuss something specific to you, your gender, class, job or other connection that people from other groups may never experience.

A an underlying frame of reference that is common between your reader and the story doesn't suffice however. There will be an element that keeps them engaged with the narrative and hooked all the way through. The most effective tool you could employ to accomplish this is tension. No matter what different emotions you incite the audience, you'll need to create some element to keep the audience guessing and curious to know what's going to transpire in the future.

The most effective way to deal with this is conflict, which refers to having something that hinders the principal person in the story either the author or another person - from reaching a goal. In order to do that, write down the goal you want to achieve or your end point at the very beginning of the tale. Find something that's hindering or hindering that objective from being achieved, even though the battle does not constitute the main aspect of the story. The problem doesn't necessarily have to involve an individual in this antagonistic job - but it's better to steer clear of doing the situation because it could be perceived as a plot to discredit the other person or elevate yourself in order to make them fall down or seem like an evil thing. For instance, a large work load with a tight date, or a challenge that, if addressed, would assist a large number of people, or even an issue with a foreign language in the country of origin.

The importance of conflict is not only in stories that are told for the sake of inspiring. Some people believe that it is not appropriate to tell stories that are intended to inspire and that talking about the difficulties which lie ahead of them on an en route will make viewers to be discouraged. The first thing to note is that not mentioning the tough parts of life is considered to be dishonest or a bit patronizing for the audience as well as it undervalues the strength of human nature. Humans are incredibly resilient when it comes to conquering challenges. Telling individuals about the challenges they might face along the way can actually inspire individuals to try to beat the obstacles by themselves.

Characters

The clear, well-defined characters make a story more compelling and give the story life. Therefore, it is important to create the characters in your story to ensure that they are as lively as they can be.

In general, you'll possess a much more in-depth experience with your character that your audience. It is your responsibility to make sure to convey that information to your audience. Make sure not to give in to the desire to provide all the details you can about the characters as you can and help readers understand each aspect of them the way you can. This is not a good idea - spending too much time establishing your characters will eat up precious time you could use to develop the plot and make your readers lose interest. Additionally, you'll not get enough time to explain them in detail, which is why don't attempt to do it.

Instead, what you need to do is to choose some of the characteristics which best define the person, and then choose one or two of them that truly distinguish them from other characters and focus on this. In order to keep the character with the viewers and make it easy for them to recognize from other characters is superior to acquiring an accurate understanding of their character as an individual.

At a minimum, you should connect one characteristic that you select to the message you are trying to convey in some manner In the case of the main persona, you'll want that particular characteristic to be one that you highlight. It is also important to locate a way to highlight that particular characteristic in your story. This can cement the idea within the minds of the audience, aiding in the imprinting of your character.

The majority of the stories you share will feature the character of you. Your character is, in the end the main participant for the tales that unfold throughout your day and the one that you are the most familiar with. Most of the time, you'll be the sole character in the story. There may be the other characters mentioned briefly, and the majority of your interaction will be with your situation. If you are telling a story in which you're the protagonist be aware the same principle that can be applied to other characters is applicable to you. Your viewers don't recognize you the way they are. Use the same strategy to portraying yourself the way the characters you portray. Make sure you portray yourself in a manner that the audience will identify with and connect with you when speaking to people who are younger such as yourself, you can talk about how you felt at your age (and without being snarky "in my day" kind of manner. Tell the truth - you weren't as confident and relaxed as they are).

Do not portray yourself as perfect or overly praising yourself. It could be seen as the sign of an exaggerated self-esteem, which can be off-putting for the majority of people. Be honest about the things you are proud of and try to appear self-deprecating. Try to make yourself seem less than your audience by a bit in the least. but in a positive way. make yourself appear like something people identify with. And perhaps secretly doubt yourself in the same way. Being apathetic, distracted or socially untidy are excellent examples. People are always reminded of the fact that they're normal for the way they behave and will also accept the person who's not flawless and has the humility to recognize the fact that they are not perfect.

Detail

A great story will take the same approach when it comes to specifics of the story like it does with the character of the story: it contains sufficient details to keep the story interesting and captivating to the viewer but without going overboard to overwhelm them, making the story boring and dull.

The first time you tell a story, it is important to establish your scene and describe the physical environment and/or emotions that the characters experience. What is required for this differs between an individual experience as well as an extended story that covers several years. In general, you'll need to explain the emotional and physical aspects for a particular situation however, with a longer span of time, you may leave out the physical aspects if the tale's subject matter is only emotionally or academic.

In order to illustrate this, when you're telling a story about the path you traveled to be a winner of the amateur beach volleyball championship You can opt to include specific details such as the court you played on and the temperatures, or decide not to. But the main point of the tale is the determination and hope that you and your team members felt throughout the tournament. If you're describing the final game However, you need to describe the court, the crowd and team colors they were sporting, the sounds and chants they were chanting and other such details and the anticipation and excitement the team and you felt.

In general, following the scene-setting, each and every detail you present to the viewers should highlight your point and move your story along. In the same vein as your final beach volleyball game, you do not have to describe each and every person on the other side, however, you could describe the centre-forward, that seemed to block a majority of your shots at first however, you soon figured her weak point - the ability to not block any ball that comes from left field and started using it to propel yourself into the victory.

Also, be aware that your target audience may not be just your closest friends who you frequently share stories with. Small details that may interest the reader may not appeal to their attention and so be wary of the desire to list more than you need to.

Step 4: Structure your narrative

Since the very first written records that we have, in the thousands of other cultures across the globe, followed a well-established and consistent pattern. Its widespread use across space and over time is a testimony to the strength and importance of stories. The pattern that stories have been following since the very beginning of the art of storytelling is the three-part arrangement: beginning, middle - ending. It is effective because it's logical and is based on the patterns that we've observed in nature. Everything we see is affected by the passage of time, from seasons and days to the life itself.

The beginning

It is here that you can get the audience's attention and present them with all the information they'll need in order to fully comprehend the plot, which is why it is essential to not be a slouch on the information. The previous article has covered the context you have to provide just enough information, but and not excessively so, but you must also concentrate on the opening.

The thing you want to do is something that immediately grabs the attention of your reader. In terms of storytelling, it is referred to as"hook" or "hook" - a line or sentence that instantly puts the stakes at a very high level. It starts right at the story - avoid for granted the "Lord of the Rings" method of starting your tale. Instead, you should begin from the infamous Shire prior to having been outside of your home. Tolkien was able to benefit from printing on paper as well as three volumes over which to share his tale. In the best case scenario it will take you between 15 and 20 minutes. Most of the time, far smaller. If there are crucial details that occur before the event, you could discuss them immediately after the hook, in flashback.

As an example, imagine that you're retelling the story of being lost in the large city while you were a child and your goal is to convey the generosity of strangers. The story doesn't start by telling your mom about your trip. It is followed by the task of packing your bags and making for the lengthy drive and the fact that you consumed way more soda than you should and needed to stop in the vehicle to pee every 5 minutes, until the time your mom ordered you to pee inside your empty Big Gulp cup you'd drank the soda from, and on. It starts with a loud and blatant statement that says,

"There I was, a six year old country boy lost in the middle of Manhattan with no idea where my mom was".

The sentence immediately grabs attention and builds tension as the audience is forced to question how you ended up to be in this situation at all This is an essential aspect that you could fill in with flashbacks immediately following - focusing on all the crucial specifics, naturally.

The middle

It is where you get the heart of the story, it's important you set the bar high all the way through. Be concise and precise in your details is crucial here. the excessive detail could disrupt the flow of your story and make your tale seem a bit stale.

One way to keep the stakes on high is by using trial-and-error cycles. A glimpse of optimism appears, increasing the expectations of the viewers but only to disappoint them in the end when they discover that it may not exactly be the way they hoped.

In our case, you notice a woman dressed as your mother and rush to her, however upon closer examination, it is revealed to not be her. You believe "she looks kind, maybe I could ask her to help me," however, you realize that her English isn't that great. It is then that she realizes the situation isn't clear and purchases candy bars to help you. She then locates the policeman. She is able to tell the officer that she's lost, and then takes you on the way to the police station. assure you of your safety and to sure you're protected. Police issue the call to find a mom who is missing her child. The call is answered quickly, however it's someone else looking for a child who is missing completely...

In the middle, you ask questions pertinent to the message you are trying to convey - do you believe this odd woman? Are you able to trust the police? The list goes on.

The end

The final step is to conclude your story, address all questions and reiterate your message or moral. You may choose to stay discreet - allowing the audience to determine what your story is supposed to reveal on their own but you could also express it clearly and directly declare the message clearly. Also, you can make your readers happy, or make them want additional information by leaving an enticing snippet from a second incident that is derived the story. For example, your mother eventually comes across you after many hours and the lady that helped you being by your side all the time. The story can be a stand-alone story and then come to your argument that there are trustworthy people around you that you can be confident in, and decide to finish the tale to a close by describing the way you and your mom leave the station and discover her vehicle, which was parked on the curb while she was trying to reach you, has removed ..."but this is a different tale."

The last method is helpful if you've talked to an audience regularly and would like to invite them to return, or to be contacted by viewers to recount what happened following the event.

Chapter 5: Telling Your Story Tips for the Stage

Finally! The moment has arrived that you learn how to prepare when the opportunity comes to perform on the stage. Your goal in telling a story is to reach your audience and impact the lives of those around them, but no whatever your tale is, it could be devalued by an inanimate performance on stage. An impressive stage presence On the other hand will definitely enhance the story more memorable and leave the impression of the minds of your audience.

The next chapter will review of how to enhance your performance on stage by making utilization of the various tools are available to you.

The stage is in the making.

There's certainly some more work to make. Preparation isn't overemphasized and the plans you need to create specifically for this stage differ from the ones you need to do when you write the story.

Make sure to keep your story in memories

There's plenty additional information that we'll be discussing with greater detail in the following chapter, but for the moment the fact that you need to perform this step is enough. It is not advisable to tell your story in a jumbled fashion on a paper - this is a hassle and will significantly limit your interactions with the viewers. It is not advisable to read your entire tale out of memory in a strict way, completely repetitive manner since that could render your presentation dull, stale and uninteresting.

What you need to create is an outline of your narrative important points that you'll write down within which you will complete the story. It allows you to be flexible in order to adjust your presentation to their reaction and be ready in case of the time you have allocated to your story being shortened because of a delay. By having an outline in place that you have prepared, you will not be frightened when something comes up.

Ideally, your outline marks will be permanently etched into your memory, so you don't need to turn for cue cards. Utilizing only memory allows the freedom to communicate with and be able to adapt to your audience. So this is definitely the best option you could perform. If you are sure that you'll need them, if you're still new to the whole public speaking process or believe you could become overwhelmed or a bit scattered, then you may want to consider allowing you to utilize the tools. Make your outline point on smaller pieces of card or a paper that is stiff and backed at a size that are able to read at arm's length You don't need to look at them to try and decipher the message you've written. If the handwriting you've written looks as if someone has dipped a squirt into ink, and then let the ink run wild on the cue card, then you'd rather print them off. However, you should try not to think about your cue cards as minimally as you can and then try to get rid of the cards as time passes.

It is possible that your speaking event will be governed by a rule that prohibits the usage of cue cards which would make the situation more settled, making you use your memory for the task regardless.

Make sure you know where to go.

Another thing to get find out the particulars of the venue. There will be a stage or do you tell your tale from the audience? Where will the people be set up - sitting in tables or rows? There will be a podium which you could stand in front of or perhaps not? What are the dimensions of the area you'll be performing in, as well as the number of people in the audience? The particulars of the location will determine the exact way you will conduct the remainder of your presentation. If you are able, figure out ways to gain access to the location - putting your self in the speaking room will give you more insight into how you can tailor your performance for it.

Look your best

If the time for the speech actually happens the time be mindful of the appearance you present. The way you dress will depend on the setting of the occasion - for instance, if you're attending a formal ceremony, it's required to dress formal (unless you're employed by an innovative startup or tech firm where you're allowed to wear a casual T-shirt) If you're bridesmaid or best man of honor for a family member's wedding, you'll wear whatever you're wearing. A theme-specific tuxedo or dress may have been selected to suit you. In most occasions where you're just telling your story and do not have an official dress code, you are able to put on whatever clothes you typically wear when you're out in public. You do wish to reflect your personality. Do not wear clothing that is distracting however -

bright patterns and colors, flashy jewellery, accessories such as sunglasses, hats and caps and other such items. They can attract the attention of your surroundings, but they distract from the message you're saying.

Begin to warm up in preparation for taking to the stage

Prior to stepping onto the stage, it is essential get yourself warm and make sure your mind is geared for the task. It is essential to maintain complete control of your body while it comes to stage performance, like we'll see in the future, which is why you must prepare your body, too. It's recommended to prepare a thorough pre-stage routine which you perform every moment you're set going to take the stage that helps get your in the proper state of mind. Meditation is an excellent beginning point There are a variety of methods you could use to choose the one that is effective well for your needs. It is also possible to do stretching and breathing exercises and warm-ups for your voice to get your voice ready for the hours during which you'll need your voice continuously.

Engaging your target audience

This is vital for you to communicate your message. Your audience must feel that they have a connection to you so that your emotions become theirs too and they are able to follow into your story with you. dive into your tale.

You are who you are.

The advice given is all over the world today, almost until it becomes cliché, yet it's just as valid. You are the person who lived through and conceived the story thus your narrative will be far more authentic when you let your personality be seen clearly.

Maintain eye contact

Eye contact is of paramount importance while performing in the stage. The eyes are a window for the soul, it is said, and your audience will be more able to connect with the emotions of your performance if you remain in eye contact. It's a common tips for public speaking which states that you must look at something in the distance of your audience members, especially when you're nervous. This evasive strategy in dealing with the causes that cause nervousness will be discussed over in the coming chapter. However, it's quite obvious to a person in the audience if you're not absconding from their attention. Take them in from the eye, and snatching the eyes of those close to you in random ways to make them sense a connection to your.

Another reason to maintain eye contact is the possibility to be aware of the reactions of your audience. It allows you to see what they're reacting to the message you're delivering and then adjust your message to their reactions. Be aware that your audience isn't your audience - you may have specific elements of your story that you've added so that they could trigger certain reactions from your audience. The audience may respond to these elements differently. For instance, a joke that you hoped was going to be hilarious may only trigger a couple of laughters, whereas one that you weren't sure was impressive could make them smile quite a bit. It's the same with any emotional reaction that you wish to trigger. This is why the ability to adapt your speech based on an outline comes to your aid - you are able to alter your presentation according to certain aspects that resonate with your people in the audience.

The tone of your voice

Your voice will be the main method you use to communicate your ideas You use your voice to convey the words of your tale Naturally. Therefore, it is crucial that you know the specifics that you use it when performing exactly right.

Enunciation and volume

In the beginning first, be sure you're heard. Your volume and the projection of your voice is vital when it comes to this. This is why preparing the venue prior to your event is helpful to prepare: If there's an audio system for public addresses that's protected, however if there aren't any, then you'll have consider the dimensions of the venue to ensure that you use your voice to speak to people who are the furthest away from you.

The pronunciation of your words is also crucial. It is essential to ensure that the words you speak aren't muddled and each syllable is clear and easy to hear and be careful not to mumble. It is important to avoid speaking at a high speed and speak in a an appropriate pace to ensure your audience can easily understand what you're talking about.

Tone

Talk naturally and casually as you would typically speak to someone in person and only adjust your voice volume so that you can reach all. Whatever feelings you want to invoke, try doing it using the same tone of voice that you use with an individual. Conversation is another method to get your message across to your target viewers - it gives them the impression that there is a connection between them and you.

Utilize your voice to help establish a mood

These points are just guidelines, fundamental rules of your discipline in singing. It is true that your voice is an incredible instrument you are able to use to trigger the feelings of the audience as well as add the weight of your speech.

The first thing to consider is tone. there are certain kinds of stories that require you to increase your tone a bit away from the natural rhythm. This is typically the case with folk stories like fairytales, myths, or legends other such tales. There is a possibility of telling your own story in this manner to make it more effective, however your ability as a storyteller will need to be quite sophisticated to be able to do it. Try not to attempt it in a formal setting as you're still developing your craft, however, you may try your hand at this with a smaller, comfortable group such as your family or a storytelling group that can offer feedback about how you're doing properly.

You can play around with your speed, volume and pitch tend to be more regular They fall under the definition that you use your voice naturally because you use them often. Utilize them to add a aspect of drama to the story you are telling - boost your pitch, voice, or volume. speak faster in order to generate suspense and make your story more suspenseful or gravity-based.

Silence

While speaking it is important to never undervalue the potential of silence. Its initial use is immediately after you get in front of the audience or take the scene. When the applause and clapping has ceased, you should take a break for a few seconds before beginning your presentation. It's an act that every professional speaker performs, from presidents to politicians, to stand-up comedians, TV hosts and so on. The silence you observe has advantages for both you and your audience. It gives you the chance to gather your thoughts, to take a deep breath before introducing your message in a strong way, as well as allowing the audience to calm and get ready to take in the message you are delivering.

Also, you should use intermissions throughout the story. This serves two reasons First, it provides you with a chance to pause and consider your ideas before going on. Secondly, it allows for the reactions of your audience. You should have set aside silences where you anticipate that the audience will respond in a loud manner, like gasps for laughter, sighs in shock, "aww's" for a sense of comradeship, cute moments, or even applause in places where you believe it should be offered. The reasons for this are that they might not be as effective as they are expected to so you need to make sure to adjust your spacing in line with the audience's reaction. Letting the reactions of your audience unfold lets them experience the emotions of their audience to its greatest extent. This also ensures the story be heard since you don't want to make yourself heard and won't be focused on something which you've gotten beyond.

It is also possible to employ silence as a way to emphasise your point as well as to give the audience to process the most complex or profound aspect that they might not understand completely if you do not give them the time they need.

Your body and your mannerisms

It is important to bear your mind in the present that the viewers will be keeping their attention on you. Their attention isn't just at what you're saying but also your physical presence too. Use that attention to your advantage by making use of your body for communication by highlighting and enhancing your message, but you must avoid behaviors which can distract or detract from the message.

Chapter 6: The facial expressions you display

It is crucial that you pay attention to them since they're the most well-known non-verbal means to express your emotions. In general, it is best to wear a pleasant and sociable smile whenever you're telling a story. If the story is swaying to both sides of the scale of emotions, then it is possible to adopt a face expression more in line of the subject - serious for more serious stories or more enthusiastic to tell a more fun, lighter tale. The story you write will be characterized by upswings and downswings in emotion but you should alter your facial expressions in line with these.

Your hands

This is another excellent tool for drawing attention to certain elements of the story. The way you utilize these tools will be contingent on whether you've got a lectern or not. If you have one, you can spend the bulk of the tale with them resting on the lectern will work however, you will require them to move to a certain extent. Releasing, waving and clenching your hands whenever necessary to create animations for the story. If you don't have the lectern available, there are two other options one of which is that either you own either a microphone, or not have one or you may be using a microphone that is a stalk or a bead. Whichever it is, it will only affect how many hands that you must deal with. A microphone that sticks to your stick could take the hands of one person for a long time. Whatever the case it is important to avoid giving your other hand(s) at you. Make use of them to emphasize, or for illustrative purposes.

Your posture

Be careful not to slouch. Your entire appearance on stage will exude confidence.

Move!

If you're performing on the stage in an open area, try not being too anchored to a single spot. Do not move too much also, as it could be distracting. It is best to choose a place that is in at the centre of the stage. each time you make a few steps left. take a moment and then move a few steps towards the right, creating the shape of a tiny, rough circle around the spot. If you're using a podium and you need to move about is eliminated as well, so you don't need to move around in the event that your location of speaking falls in the middle of the audience.

Practice

The importance of practice is not just in creating your perfect story for stage. Technically, it's an important aspect of getting ready for your show, but there are some aspects that must be a reference to the things we spoke about in the preceding section, and also have been reintroduced here to be considered in relation.

It is important to use practice to test different methods as you gain confidence and refine the story you tell. In this article, we will discuss the three major elements of practicing and the things they are. Do your practice wherever and whenever you want Some of the tips mentioned will require certain setting and equipment that must be in place, but they're not required constantly. Do it whenever you can find enough opportunity.

1. Practice!

This is of course the very first aspect you must do to practise your speaking. It won't be enough to simply repeat it over and over again in your mind and you will need to perform it and loud. There are several benefits when you read your story loudly First of all, you'll get comfortable making use of your voice in telling your story. Speaking out the story you've written is different than reliving the story in your head as you try to get used to it in order to avoid having to do it the first time once you step onto the stage.

The other benefit is connected to the first There are words or phrases that seem good in your head but might not be impressive when you say them out loud. It is also possible to find phrases that can be unintentionally tongue-twisters, poetically gorgeous and appealing, but difficult to pronounce. It is possible to try taking the challenge However, it's better to stay away from making your vocabulary simple, particularly when you're just getting started.

Also, you don't talk in the same way as you believe. Making the effort to tell your story and loud helps you gauge your time better. This also allows you to determine how speaking your story loudly actually makes your feel. It could certain parts of your story that will be more emotionally charged when you read them aloud but you shouldn't wish to fall victim to them.

Additionally, it helps in figuring out the technical problems you might face in your story This process will carry on throughout the time you share your tale.

It is possible to begin with reading the story exactly as you've written the entire story, however after a few repetitious readings, start to work in telling your story using your outline. Move from your full-length outline to more concise bullet points before moving to your outline before finally eliminating the outline entirely. It is possible to carry them when you perform for backup purposes, however, you must aim at being able to tell the story in your own words.

Practice standing up. This is especially important when you'll be telling your story at the time of the event. This can assist you in establishing the mindset you'll require to enter at the story's end, as sitting also affects the way you move and your voice projection. Also, you should do the exact moves you'll be performing during the performance, as this can help develop muscle memory which is in tune with the words.

Also, you should try to prepare in the venue the venue will be during the time you deliver your speech. If you're able to be in the exact space, then that would be a great thing. If not, you can settle for making it look in the best way you can, in a comparable space. It is crucial to duplicate the stage's layout make sure you choose a venue which is similar in size to the stage. If you're using an instrument, locate it to play with or if you've got an audio system, locate one alternatively, use a similarly-sized round object.

2. Be aware of your own behavior

It's difficult to know precisely how you'll appear or sound when speaking to someone else It's crucial to have an perception of your appearance on the outside. One method in order to do this is practice the mirror. Becoming able to observe your reflection will allow you to improve the physical aspect of the performance. Be aware of the posture of your face, facial expressions and movements to determine how others might perceive them.

Also, you should record your own narration. Voices are particularly hard to discern the tone from outside because your ears get benefit from the resonance created by the skull. It is not a pleasant experience to listen to voices recorded at the beginning, but over time you'll become accustomed to the sound and become better equipped to determine if you're making use of it after just some initial listening. When you are comfortable with the technology, you'll become more adept at being able to determine and adjust the level, tone, volume and speed to your highest levels. Additionally, you will be at identifying phrases and words which sound off or don't pronounce them correctly. This can help in helping you to comprehend the tale when you listen to it repeated over and over again, the story will be able to stay in your head more effectively.

The essence of these two concepts by recording video of your own speech. The video is even better than a mirror since it allows you to look at your own performance without having the stress and stress of having to remember and share the story. It will give you a perspective which someone else might be unable to. The process of recording yourself isn't difficult at all in the present. Today, you do not require the cinematic qualities of your smartphone -

its microphone and camera can do perfectly.

3. Get feedback

Although the last section gives you an outside view, it is likely that you remain a bit naive about you and your work. There will be other people to look at the performance of yours and offer an objective view of it. Choose a group of people to present your message to at least one from the same age group as the actual audience.

There's more than just encouragement that the audience is looking for Ask to receive honest and precise comments on what they thought of the narrative as well as how they feel, which aspects that you performed put off them, details on your vocal and appearance, as well as general suggestions on how to make improvements. A live audience will aid in getting used to performing before a crowd of people that is quite different than performing in front of an empty space or wall.

Overcoming Fear and Learning To Love The Stage

The fear of speaking in public is among the most frequently feared fears being a step above phobias like spiders, heights and death. It is likely that you're among the millions who are afraid of public speaking. Even If you're not studying, you don't know when you might aid someone else.

For a better understanding of the fear associated with public speaking, let's have the time to look at its origins it's anxiety about failing and causing the wrong impression when speaking in front of crowds and could result in the loss of one's social standing as well as a decline in the ability of wooing an acquaintance. Ironically evident that often it's the fear of failure that leads to the loss through the primal "fight or flight" response and diverts energy from thinking and can cause physical movements.

Some well-meaning folks have attempted to offer "remedies" to this fear. You've probably been told to stand at the crowd's heads and wear a charm that represents luck and remind yourself that it will be soon over, or even imagine the crowd without clothing. These all have something in common and that is the idea of avoiding - getting your mind away from the anxiety or rid of the situation. It is not helpful as your fear is likely to remain and cause unwanted effects.

The best thing a solution to fear is control the fear once it comes up rather than avoiding it. Then, eventually conquer it until it's no longer an problem. Learn to let go of fearing the stage and to accept and enjoy the stage.

The most important thing to think about whenever you are given a piece of advice is: What can it accomplish? Can it help me overcome my fear or assist me in managing and conquer the fear? This same inquiry can be applied to all the behaviors you are engaging in when you're anxious. The goal is not to just cover or distract you from your anxiety but should actually help to overcome it.

In this article, we will examine what you have to be doing during the three stages of preparation: setting up the stage, and finally the end.

1. Preparation

Keep your hat on hold on tight, because what I'm going to share with you will shock you. The foremost thing you should perform during your preparation to reduce your anxiety is to practice! The steps in the earlier section will do a lot in your confidence. You will be able to understand the material from top to bottom Find any niggles which could cause you to inadvertently stumble, and become comfortable in the setting and concept of speaking in front of the crowd.

A couple of other options which also harken on previous chapters. Learn to tell stories. They enhance your skills overall and the confidence that you know something is a huge boost to confidence. Speaking about something that you're enthusiastic about can also help to make your story more compelling, and so linking it into a story that is profoundly impacting for you, and which you want to pass on to other people is an ideal concept.

2. The stage

Beating the fear of speaking on stage is also a matter of preparing before you get ready to talk. Preparing for your performance with a ritual prior to the event is an ideal idea which even masters use. You can tailor it to your needs and move, do some easy exercises, or just sit in meditation. If you're still feeling tension, make use of this opportunity to redirect on excitement. Fear and anticipation are both part of the same hormone pathway and all it requires from your mind is a positive outlook one that views what's coming as an opportunity instead of as an inconvenience to endure.

As you step onto stage Pay attention to your breathing. It's common to fail to breathe in the right way. Utilize your time in silence to breathe a deeply breathe that cleanses your lung. Inhaling deeply increases the flow of oxygen to your brain, enhancing your concentration as well as flushing the fear-causing hormones.

Remember all the tips provided in the 4th chapter keep in mind, and avoid talking too quickly. Speeding up will make you fall, adding the stress.

3. Afterwards

After the event is finished It is important to celebrate your achievement before going to analyzing mode. Be thankful it's done, but be grateful that you were able to tell your story. If you were a bit anxious, feel proud of having faced the issue head on. Recollect the happy reactions, as well as the instances when you got people to respond in the manner you intended they would.

After you've completed that take note of the results as a prelude to the next event and start to put your focus to this. Make any mistakes you make as a lesson to learn from and strive to be better the next time around. The event itself can be quite different from all the bits of work you've put in until now So if you are able to obtain a video of your performance then examine it. Find areas that you want to get better at and work on in the future when you have to tell a story using the same ideas to keep them in your mind.

Chapter 7: HYPNOTIC HERO'S JOURNEY

HYPNOTIC HERO'S

JOURNEY

The later Joseph Campbell learnt the common thread that is prevalent in all stories and epics. The story begins with a typical background, only to be abruptly broken by sudden interruption in the story, which, then the story begins to unfold; that ultimately circles towards the place where it originally began. This story structure has a beginning with a captivating and captivating adventure. This is why it is the place to begin.

At age nineteen, I contacted my dad to see to accompany his truck (he was a truck driver) for him to deliver the freight. I was mainly interested in seeing America. United States of America and several other places that I had not had the privilege of visiting. It was always a pleasure to travel.

Every day, I was being awoken in a different place. It could take place in Minneapolis, Minnesota one morning or Saint Louis, Missouri the next day, and Fort Myers, Florida another and so on. It all was contingent upon the schedule of my father.

There were times when it was very cold extremely cold, with temperatures below 0degrees Fahrenheit. At other times, it was extremely extremely hot, hot to the point of being at or above 100deg F. But the point is that it was different every time I found it to be amazing.

After travelling with him for long periods of time, I began to feel anxious at times, and then. I nearly became bored. There was a lot in my head, considering I was still young, and thinking concerning my future, and the things I wanted to get out of my life. I was unsure about this, and I was worried. The time seemed to go by more quickly and quicker with the progress of every single month. The year was coming to an end.

I began to read.

The book that I found to be hypnotically fascinating was Ramayana of Valmiki. The story is an epic Hindu epic, in which the main character Rama is removed from his home and is forced to be a recluse for 14 years within the forests on the edge of his kingdom. His wife Sita as well as his brother Lakshmana were with the king. Another brother Bharat governs in his absence.

Rama's day is normal till his spouse Sita discovers that one day she has been captured by the wicked demon King Ravana.

Rama has to travel southwards to Lanka in order to find her.

At the end, he is successful and finally is able to regain his kingdom.

The tale is a great illustration of Campbell's "Hero's Journey The reason is that it covers every aspect of, or the majority of the things that Campbell considers as true in the majority of epics and myths.

Since this is the base narrative, it's important to begin by examining the hero's hypnotic journey so that you can grasp the underlying meaning of a hypnotic tale.

Why the Hypnotic Hero's Journey?

The journey of a hypnotic hero is the ultimate story that we imagine and remember right from the beginning of our journey. Our lives mirror the hypnotic heroes' travels, but in reality. It begins with an entry into the world, which seems common and ordinary in the slightest. We then experience a type change, like coming to maturity or some similar event. After that, we begin the journey of self-discovery, and personal development. Then we discover our real essence. We discover what we're capable of? The way we learn is through experience; in order to find the truth about ourselves, and also to discover our path in our own way. In this course, we go through difficulties and trials, and the lessons learned from these experiences help us grow stronger and more wise. In the end, we discover our way and discover the meaning of our lives that has been handed to us and discover our purpose or dharma, then strive to achieve this. After achieving it, we come back to our old, familiar and the place where we started, so to complete the circle around us.

You can see that the "hypnotizing hero's story" is one that we recognize and identify with as being pertinent to our particular lifestyle. It's the isomorphic connections in these stories which address our own internal issues which we are unable to resolve. These metaphors about our own lives are hypnotic because they reveal the essence of what it takes being human.

What is the Hypnotic Hero's Journey?

Like I've mentioned that the journey of the hypnotic hero is an analogy to the human experience, specifically how it feels to exist as a human, in this world of human beings. Everyone has their individual experiences that we have. Certain certain aspects of our life that are reflected within the lives of other people. The hero's journey of hypnosis is a classic representation of the traditional story, which begins in a normal life, but then transforms to a thrilling adventure initially unpredictable and it reaches its peak at a certain point or climax with intense emotion, and eventually, it reaches some sort of conclusion that eventually brings us back to the place where the archetype of a hypnotic hero's journey was first introduced, i.e. normalcy. This is an endless cycle of denigration that could stop us in our tracks and inspire ourselves to demonstrate our own worth and the things we're capable of accomplishing despite being criticized by others, and the things they think of us and all of which add up to a variety of events in life.

The well-known author Paulo Coelho; author of The Alchemist, stated how his parents dissuaded him from becoming writers, preferring his career as an engineer similar to his father. In the event that he did not, the idea, his parents went as in a way as to make him taken to a mental institution. They knew they wanted only the ideal to him, he ultimately accepted a law degree and then left one year later, for a more private journey that ultimately brought him back to the writing profession. The experiences he had; that's the journey of defiance and ignoring what other people had made for him and choosing to pursue his own individual path, brought him to the ultimate achievement as a well-known writer.

As you can see, the mythic hero's journey provides an incredible learning experience, however as is the uncertainness of whether you'll be successful or fail in the process, as well as a departure the expectations we're placed on ourselves as well as what's familiar and the comfort zone 3/4 in place of an alien and unknown journey which has attracted us to a feeling of awe wherein we are swept into a and deep and trance. The experience can be frightening yet it can be educational, as well as is the reason we feel happy and awe as well as the testing of the faith we have. There are also advantages, like riches, love of power and friendships that are yet to be found.

According to Campbell Campbell, this form of hero's quest has also been dubbed the "Monomyth due to it being the thread common to all myths and is the basis of almost every epic and mythological poem across the ages.

How to Tell the Hypnotic Hero's Journey?

Once we've figured out the meaning behind it and how it's an essential narrative of the many stories we share, that we are aware of the importance of the hypnotic journey or that we've got enough knowledge and knowledge to begin at a point where we can narrow it down for us to create our own hero's journey hypnotic stories. This section will outline the basics of Campbell's Monomyth framework that will help you to quickly present your own Hypnotic Hero's Journey at any time or anywhere, instantly and effortlessly!

The Call to Adventure

It's important to remember that we begin by describing the normal, everyday, or, in some cases, boring. This is the everyday routine that someone, the protagonist in the story i.e. the main character, understands and relies upon for the purpose of assuming an identity that is unique to them. As I think about it, I see the situation as one of a collective controlled life which the protagonist is born to. I'm reminded of an Indian child who was born into a family of collectivists that has grandparents living alongside parents who reside alongside children. Everybody is responsible for everyone other person, and everyone is assigned an agenda, and a sense of identity that encompasses the whole family unit.

The desire to explore is an invitation to leave the collective identity towards an individual identity that's separated away from the familial unit 3/4 toward the mystery that defines our individuality. There is a division from the family unit, as you'll observe.

The way in which the desire to explore results in a different from story to tale. The emergence of adventure can happen quite abruptly and random 3/4the most unlikely possibility or it could be planned in advance and developed in the course of time, should you wish. It is the responsibility of the storyteller who is hypnotized to choose the way it happens.

It is the creative aspect that plays an important role in the calling to take action. It is usually a rousing event that helps set the scene for the adventure. The adventure is the greatest escape, or even the greatest anticipation, or even the greatest expectations that go wrong.

The Refusal of the Call

Sometimes, however and often, the character is hesitant to accept the challenge of adventure. Sometimes the character is reluctant to embark on the adventure. The reason for this can come from various reasons. (a) the character is pushed by the circumstances to stay at a location that is safe and accepted, and occasionally the responsibilities of his environment can be more persuasive over the inner desire to leave and set out to seek a new future. In this case then the character in question may feel a sense of dissonance within and wonder, "What might have been?"

In the end, tensions may escalate until the need for a break-up is required in which case the protagonist surrenders to the dictates of fate, agreeing to let go of what is required from him in order to take on the trip regardless. At times the character must take the difficult decision to sacrifice his own life as a result of an ultimatum to take on the challenge. It can lead the reader, i.e. the subject of the hypnotic story to be totally absorbed in the narrative.

The Supernatural Aid

Campbell's final element in his hero's journey involves the introduction of an aid supernatural, which helps the hero in one manner by providing him or the hero with advice and perhaps an item that can assist to cross the first hurdle, aiming to prevent the hero from entering the next world, where the journey officially starts.

Recalling the tale of the Bhagavad Gita. It is an Indian spiritual work where the hero, Arjun must battle his brothers during a battle of epic proportions, since it is his duty fighting, as a result of having been born in the Kshatriya classes The parallel I see as Lord Krishna offering consoling advice to Arjun and giving him reasons to fight in the battle he initially isn't willing to take on. There is no better tale in which murder is seen as a noble choice, portrayed to the reader as exemplary and unrepentant, as well as Godly.

This short tale is an excerpt is taken from the most epic poem ever written, that is The Mahabharata, the supernatural aid actually a incarnation of God that is also Arjun's charioteer in the story of Arjun. This is an incredibly hypnotic tale 3/4 I strongly recommend.

It is a secondary character in numerous epic and mythological stories. The character could appear to appear right moment to help the protagonist by a significant way. The character I am thinking of is a metaphor for the unfathomable power of the universe to assist and support individuals on their journey. Sometimes, it's us that have to help the character listen to and learn from their individual or refuse the assistance they offer, which typically, comes in adverse consequences which affect your journey's success.

The supernatural figure is usually known as the "voice of reason" that helps to inform the protagonist as well as to assist in maturing him/her as well as prepare them to face the challenges to come. The character in question is older, wise and often elderly person, one who can be a hypnotic signification for discernment and wisdom. If we are the readers or listener to this sort of tale you may find yourself unconsciously relating to this particular character as an adult figure or as a wise grandmother that always tries to protect us from risk, and prepare our minds for the dangers that may be encountered along the way of our lives, so in order to avoid falling into these traps and complications.

The First Threshold

After leaving to explore what lies ahead, the character demonstrate their worthiness by crossing into the world that is unknown. This land of mystery is guarded from the guardianship of a. The archetype of the guardian is the very first step by where the character must show the worthiness of their character to continue with carrying off of their journey.

The "unknown" that is guarded by this guardian symbolically hypnotically a representation of the 'other' also known as the "unconscious mind' The guardian archetype hypnotically represents of the 'critical faculties' which functions as a filter, allowing certain sensory data in, but blocks other sensory information to be absorbed by the mind..

From the perspective of hypnotic storytelling These hypnotic images are crucial to know, since they're metaphors for the process of hypnosis, which happens when a hypnotic storyteller presents a hypnotic narrative either as a metaphor or a teaching story.

If the story reaches the threshold that is first, this becomes an isomorphic metaphor in an aspect, observing the exaggeration of the loss of the subject's cognitive faculties. When this occurs it is the time to enter the state of hypnosis, in which suggestions can be made and without fear rejection.

The Belly of the Whale

When you cross the first threshold, the protagonist is removed from his or her reality and is able to return. The character is now sucked in a new reality that is a different existence, but one that is a mystery and magical, mythical illusionary, dream-like, and illusory.

Let's think about the story for a second. As I think about this part of the tale I'm reminded of an unrealized dream and memories of my childhood when imaginations are wild and wild and unbroken like a horse which refuses to be broken and compelled to conform to the rules of the game.

Because of this, stories make the ideal method for using hypnosis because they let us go to childhood times, when we were safe and secure from all the worries and anxieties adulthood brings and where we could play with pretend, make-believe and even create as well as use our imaginations in an unpractical way. It's okay to have fun, but the same is true of mental experience. This way, we are able to be inspired and inspire to build, protect and even demolish the world as we wish and knowing that anything can be done, and that everything is able to be revived to the Samsara of our inner world in my name, the "Other Mind'.

Refusing to think about what was happening from the beginning to today The world we live in is metaphorical for our every everyday life. The transition into the world of tomorrow, i.e. the stomach of the whale, can be symbolic of the unconscious as well as the state of will be experienced when you are hypnotized.

The Road of Trials

In the present world the main character must confront various challenges. He or she must conquer obstacles that hinder their progress towards the desired boon. In Paulo's The Alchemist, the boon was the prize that the young shepherd boy was looking to find, and at last, he set off on his adventure. To discover the legend of his own, and to find the treasure that he was searching for the shepherd boy Santiago must have overcome a number of difficulties along his way. The trials made it simple for him to for a return to the routine of being a shepherd, not thinking about the difficulties he'd faced, which made the man want to forget about his own personal story.

Trials are metaphors to describe problems.

In the event that a potential client or a potential client or anybody else whom we come across who is struggling, and is seeking assistance, often best approach to assist the person is to provide them with an Isomorphic Metaphor that solves the problem of a person. This way it allows the subconscious mind of that person is able to access resources that the conscious mind would not have thought of. The spark of insight and inspiration occurs in the form of magic.

It is interesting to think that a fairy tale will solve your problem but, despite that all the smart thinking that exists could fail an individual. Interesting, isn't it?

In a epic of religious significance, problems can get blown far beyond its scope and the resolution a colossal exercise in endurance and inconceivable magnitude and proportion Take care that it could encourage you to find a solution with great strength and ability to never stop solving your own seemingly impossible difficulties. In fact, think about it briefly: perhaps the issues you face today are seen as a breeze; capable of being solved by a small fractions to. If you believe that everything is possible this makes the issues appear less significant as you originally thought they were.

An issue that is solved appears small in comparison to the other issues, or perhaps even unimportant for some situations. My college memories are vivid. I aspired to graduate with at least a 4.00 GPA. Every class seemed to be as a huge obstacle that stood between me and my dream. Each day I defeated all the monsters. After I was able to graduate with the 4.00 GPA, I reflected and thought "It really wasn't as brutal as I made it out to be, at first thought." My view had changed. But how would I perceive students who are fresher than my graduation? Are the trials more significant than what they face in real life? Yes, I believe so.

The trip isn't only the arduous trail that must be negotiated It also offers the chance to experience beauty unnoticed that are not known, and the moments of awakening spiritually can make the trip worth it's cost It is possible to one could.

The meeting with the goddess

The zenith is the story that could cause goose bumps on your face; it's a point in the tale that the main character encounters an awe-inspiring divine force that provides him with more strength and an overall strength to be in a position to fulfill the demands of the mission through to the end. It is an inner strength, derived from an underlying divine motivation to complete the last task that is awaiting the hero or heroine.

If the hero is a person, the person who is divinely portrayed symbolized as a female divinity. When a woman is a heroine, the divine being is usually depicted as a masculine divinity. It's usually the weak element that keeps heroes from having the most self-confidence and power that is personal. If the hero has a union with God, she's transformed into immortality in a metaphorical sense.

It's something that is gone, and is being discovered as a part of us which energizes us and brings our attention back on the task that is in front of us. This is an internal power that is expressed in the form of a character.

This archetype can be very hypnotic by nature because she represents our innermost spirituality which is the True Nature of us. Once your client is aware of the archetype within them, through the hypnotic tales you tell them there is a jolt that is triggered that shakes the ground under the subject and makes them discover something that is so profound, it permanently alters them in the majority of cases.

Woman as the Temptress

Be careful not to get confused thinking it's about gender. this isn't. The typical woman who is a temptress usually is female, however it does not have to be. The lure of a temptress is the simple attraction of people, objects, as well as places that are attempting to block obstacles to the pursuit of goal, i.e. what we are trying to achieve.

The story of the novel by Coelho The Alchemist this could be the young Bedouin girl that Santiago is in the love of. The beauty of her eyes alone entices him and he even thinks about abandoning his plans. This archetype can be seen in numerous other myths and epics to look into.

It is true that it is just a brief satisfaction that is ensnared to, but there is no lasting value from it, just short-term value.

In many ways, this archetype is used to assess the purity and power of the protagonist to see the extent to which they can continue on and complete the mission. A few are lured by such falsehoods.

A parallel might represent a cherished relationship that two couples vow to preserve and yet will be destined when one of them violates the vow of eternal love in exchange for a momentary satisfaction with an acquaintance that ends the connection permanently. It's a test of affection and the character of a person.

The Atonement of the Father.

The father is a symbol of the control. In a variety of tales the father figure is behind the heroine or hero taking over and sitting at the front of the table literally speaking.

The father-son relationship typically is one of tension. The relationship is often the result of rivalry as well as a struggle for recognition and power.

Atonement for the father is fighting back against the father, and in certain instances, reconciling the relationship by recasting it into a new perspective, one that is based on equal power or transference. Atonement by the father may also mean restitution of an idea or ideal that is a hindrance for the success of the hero/heroine in the coming years.

Atonement for the father In some tales, atonement of the father could be an act of rebellion against God or another godlike being. This way, atonement for the father could be the test of manhood or even a sign of maturation and independence.

The Apotheosis

The woman who is a temptress as well as an atonement for the father are two instances of challenges the protagonist needs to be able to overcome. The above trials, as well as others, raise the protagonist to an elevated status. The term apotheosis literally means into a state of elevation similar to the gods. However, in our stories of hypnosis, it may actually mean an level in which the protagonist is strengthened so that they are able to complete the difficult task ahead; that is, the big mission. It is also one of the toughest trials to be faced.

In a lot of storylines, the principal persona may be depicted differently which makes this aspect important. The Karate Kid, part 1 in which the main character Daniel Laruso, is given the headband following having suffered the retribution of being swept off his leg by the opponent. Then, he's ready to take on him head-on and performs the infamous Crane Kick that wins him the title of victory.

Chapter 8: The Ultimate Boon

The most enduring blessing is the one that the protagonist risked his life and limbs to attain. It's not just an actual object, magical elixir of life, a alchemy formula, or something else that people would be willing to sacrifice for when they thought they would achieve it. Instead it's as a symbol of character and strength, a symbol that represents the entire experience. It's a prize in numerous ways that represent the perseverance, as well as the relationship that the main character has to confront and overcome. Also, it represents transformation as well as success. This is the main reason it is more than its value. it. It is a symbol of inherent value that is far greater than what any other human being would assign to it.

Daniel Laruso believed it was an emblem of doing what was impossible. It also served as being a representation of his destruction of fear which denied his of the things was he sought. The story of Santiago In The Alchemist is was symbolic of his life and also an expression of his change from being just a shepherd child to the true alchemist. For the main character, the significance of the final boon is unimaginable. The value of the boon provides proof of the qualities that heroes are composed of and can't be destroyed.

In many cases, when people recall the most memorable moment of their life, it is often associated with this achievement, which is an ultimate reward which is their ultimate symbol of self-worth. It is possible to watch their face be animated, their tone become a roar of enthusiasm as they gain a power that's tied to the moment 3/4as if that they're experiencing the same experience over and over time.

While you're telling the hero's journey of hypnosis when you reach the final part of the story, the mind of another begins to form parallel connections to similar experiences experienced by the person being hypnotized. This could be a conscious awareness when they interrupt to talk about the same experience they've had and it could occur as an unconscious awareness that is apparent to you the subject when you look at the way they behave non-verbally.

There is a certain fact that the subjects in a profoundly emotional way. The constant reverberation of emotions that will not stop, is creating changes in their minds which is extraordinarily motivating and empowering. They are able to alter their mental state and, in turn, is likely to influence their actions as well as the kinds of choices they'll take at some point in the future. They will make decisions that are assured, solid and unwavering; directed towards your goal, and that should be in line with your direction that you're directing to.

Individuals who are scared of changing, afraid of making a decision, or who are hesitant to take risks are free of this condition, and will be more likely to follow the same path you've mentally created by hypnotizing them with your narrative.

The Refusal of the Return

The reader must imagine two distinct worlds: (a) the world in which the hero/heroine is and is referred to as the normal world as well as (b) as well the brand new universe; that which transformed him/her, elevated and elevated him/her to the level of something greater than. When we reach this point in the tale, the character will usually be required to return an opportunity to return to the world where he/she first came to with the intention of improving humanity. However, the principal persona, who is now elevated, might not want to go back to his old existence.

This leads to an enigma in the sense that the fact that the character was not able to go back to the past initially, but now does not want to leave the world of today. The parallel is happening to the character and, in many ways, the similar emotions are carried. The protagonist is now an individual who is recognized by other people and is a distinct persona; prior to that, he/she was a part of the community and the communal qualities have their own distinct value. The situation places the principal person in a dilemma where the normal reaction is to avoid returning to home.

The Magic Flight

It's not always the case, however it could be the boon is worth it and is so fervently protected by a particular group or gods that the heroes must come up with an escape strategy to make it clear of danger.

The greater the value of the boon is, the greater the likelihood that the primary protagonist will have to look for the boon and himself. Other people will also be quick to accept the boon, particularly when the main character has defeated an actual threat which had been a guardian for a long time but now, the threats which lurk aren't able to see the character as threat. It may provide an opportunity for those who are seeking the blessing to claim control of it.

This could add an additional layer of vexation and intrigue to the story as well as a surprising end, though one that could be extremely unpleasant to your viewers or the subject.

The Rescue From Without

The possibility is that, when your protagonist escapes from the dangers that are lurking may result in being injured or severely wounded. It's a little ironic in that just as the main character needed to get wise counsel as well as support when entering the new world, that same person may require assistance to leave the world to return to his or her normal life.

If this happens, the main character, after fighting the adversary, i.e. the arch enemy, will receive some assistance from someone or somewhere which will lead him or her safely back to his home. This can be a wonderful way to return to normalcy particularly since the protagonist might not wish to move on from the present for the sake of returning to home. It could also be the reason to reunite her with her past.

In the motion film"The Wizard of OzDorothy hits her heels in her ruby red slippers. She is back in her to her home as though it's just been dreams 3/4, possibly questioning the reality of Oz, the entire new realm of Oz overall.

There are so many inventive methods to take the person back to the real world, or back to the past normal world that it could create a truly memorable experience for your crowd. While you share your captivating stories, bear this in mind as it is possible that inspiration will come your way as you relate these tales. It is also possible to see the different ways of ending the subject.

The goal is to get the result of your tale that you want to achieve. Most of the time, this is to get the hypnotic subject comply to your post-hypnotic instructions.

The Crossing of the Return Threshold

The return threshold has exactly the same importance just as the entrance or first threshold. The difference is the fact that, instead of being a symbolic entering into the unexplored "other" mind, the hero is back in the daily world of consciousness that symbolizes security, home and reconnecting with his familiar. Reentry back into the home zone will mean a return into reality for the protagonist or heroine.

Some stories end with an epic battle just before the protagonist leaves the world of new and goes back to the world of where he or she came from.

After returning, the metamorphosis generally only understood by the main character, as is the case in The Wizard of Oz where Dorothy returns to Kansas. The family members didn't know or appreciate the transformation that took place within Dorothy and her family, however she understood. The process can be challenging adjustment for the character and sometimes the protagonist could be seen as unpopular and/or suffer a major mental distress that triggers depression to befall the protagonist.

I'm reminded by a trip I took on my own. I had just left in the United States and ventured off into India when I was in my teen years. I travelled on my own, having a strong spiritual desire to travel there. I went on the full spectrum of the hero's adventure as I traveled through a different country and undergoing a significant shift during my time there. After returning, people saw me the way I was when I went away, and that differed from the person who was watching me at the time. I was sucked into a deep despair, yearning to be again in India I felt like I had lost touch from a small part of me.

This was many years ago; the reason I am telling this story is to highlight the argument Jesus is making when he states that in the New Testament:

"A prophet is not without honour, but in his own country, and among his own kin, and in his own house." 3/4Jesus

People only have the persona that they meet within your workplace. Your colleagues in the modern world view the person in only one way and character, while those who were in your old company perceive you in the same way as when you first left. It's a fascinating thing if you get the chance to see it.

The Master of Two Worlds

A lot of hypnosis concerns with the idea of an the inner and outer realms, specifically, the mind as well as the 'other mind' also known as 'conscious mind' or "unconscious mind". The "hypnotic" journey of a hero represents this ability to master both worlds.

When you're a hypnotic storyteller, you're able to take people into and out of unconscious and conscious states, also known as fractionation. Every time you take people back to their old world and then to the new it is essentially removing them of hypnosis, and returning to reality.

Naturally, hypnosis occurs during the course of 90 to 120 minutes throughout our day which is known as circadian rhythms. In this time, we are drifting into a trance or daydreaming. This is a way to escape our conscious and back into the 'other' mind or the unconscious mind.

Through a narrative in which the protagonist is made to realize these two sides of himself/herself as equal 3/4 mastering each! Humans are conditioned to go through stories and be immersed in these worlds. Psychology of persuasion "Narrative Transportation Theory' is this particular method through which we take on the character's identity and identify with the main persona. It is the moment when we leave our world of consciousness and enter the unknown in order to live a life that is different from the familiar and well-known.

They are naturally hypnotic. however, when a person who is hypnotized tells stories, they add additional layers of hypnotic manipulations, the spectators, i.e. the subjects you hypnotize are placed in a state of hypnosis in the sense that you can connect with them at different levels, and meet specific goals for outcomes.

There are numerous benefits of the art of hypnotic storytelling. (a) they establish a strong relationships, (b) they communicate indirectly without provoking suspicion or apprehension, (c) they suspend judgements, (d) they allow the ability to speak clearly and with a style that people can enjoy listening to as well as (e) allow you to be hypnotized without having to be aware that they're receiving hypnosis.

According to me, the art of hypnotic storytelling is among the most intriguing methods by using which you can manipulate others. Its hypnotic quality and the way it is told in stories makes them my favorite methods of hypnotizing my clients in secret. While I was in sales, I heard an old cliche "Facts fail; stories sell!" It simply means that the people purchase the psychological benefits which are gained through the using the stories they hear or tell from sales professionals instead of logic-based benefits, i.e., facts on the characteristics that a product has.

Stories are shared with the children in our earliest years as you're being soothed into sleep by parents. It's it's a type of hypnosis for children as a method. When a child is in a loving parent's arms you are surrounded by stories to divert our mind from external and real-life activities which is a way of disconnected from the reality of our lives while being rocked into asleep, in a rhythmic manner, through the sound of parents' bouncing around in their arms as well as the soft whispered phrases that accomplish our minds what an academic's monotone tone will do: induce us to a sleep-like state that you'll find yourself in a state of hypnosis when we go to bed at night. "Sweet dreams!" may be the last thing that we hear, but they're probably asleep before we can actually be able to hear these words. The truth is, telling stories is beneficial for many reasons.

The Freedom to Live

The last element of Campbell's "Hero's Journey". The hypnotic storyteller will find this is the final dimension of the story's classic which serves as the basis on which they can later build to the story with hypnotic elements (e.g. the hypnotic language pattern, embedded command and so on.).

The final element is a sign of liberation for the character of the main character. Hero/heroine can change between the two worlds they wish. When they have mastered the art acquired through experiences, the hero/heroine can be a teacher or guide to young adventurers. They possess the expertise and skills to instruct other people about the worlds of two and also to motivate and spread the word about both.

The story could become over the course of time into a myth, or an epic tale transmitted from one generation to the following generation. This way, the hero can be elevated by the other characters to the rank of god. In this way, the hero becomes a person who is revered by the next generation of young people who want to attain that same position.

The storyteller who hypnotizes will need to know this in detail in telling the hypnotic tale, this section is likely to inspire hope and possibilities within the mind of the subject, specifically that person who hasn't met yet with the personal story of their life. It is a myriad of ways that this is a reason to motivate your audience member to be proactive and, in turn, will serve as an incentive that will make them want the action to be taken - and within this frame of mind it is possible to put any action forth 3/4 for example and the result you want to them, and the result will be complied with.

What If You Are Unable to Remember All of This Straightaway?

I would like to remind you not to worry about learning the entire 17 steps in Campbell's "Hero's Journey It's not required for you to complete the entire process. The recognition of the common thread which connects all tales is the most important thing to teach you the model.

My reworking of the model and renamed it "The Hypnotic Hero's Travel' is intended to show you the symbolic symbols of the hypnotic procedure and the way I perceive hypnosis to mean experientially. This is similar to the removal of the critical faculties where the persona represents the subject of hypnosis by avoiding the critical thought process, choosing instead to let go of doubt, opting to make the leap of faith and surrender their inhibitions and take a risk to enter the "unknown or 'unknown'. This is an image of the 'other brain as well as the emotional mind as well as what many consider to be the "unconscious brain". To me I will refer to this as the 'other brain also known as the hypnotic brain'. There are so many similarities that I've pointed out and it's enough to just generalize these similarities.

The instant you are in of the moment, you, as a learner must be aware of the parallels that exist between an'story' and the concept of the concept of hypnosis.. I'm from the school belief that learning happens through heuristics and is initially learned 'unconsciously' that, over time, is absorbed by analyzing or "consciously". What I'm trying to suggest is that you have already gained this understanding through your subconscious experiences, having shared several stories that you've learned by using the model. In order to be honest, The 'Hypnotic Hero's Journey in addition to knowing that you are aware of it.

The Recap

The chapter walked you through the monomyth, which was developed in the work of Joseph Campbell, from his book The Hero with a Thousand Faces. It is the most well-known story narrative that is prevalent in many epic stories and myths.

I have adapted the original concept in order to present to readers the hypnotic connections that established the the hypnotic storytelling tradition. The hypnotic structure hero's quest bridges the conscious, critical mind into the mysterious world of the subconscious mind. The crossing is akin to the induction of hypnosis. When you reach the point where the journey, the critical faculty has to be cleared, which is in line with Campbell's "First Threshold" step. Once the critical faculty is bypassed, the process commences, in our scenario, the hypnosis in the which the 'hypnotic brain' is guided through the imagination of the person who is hypnotized and their the ability to make up stories and play with their own mind. The guiding process of this is similar to the way in which a story is that is told from one stage from one step to the next. While the person being hypnotized is by a long trip of secret and excitement, but it is not conscious of having to go anywhere.

www.ingramcontent.com/pod-product-compliance
Lightning Source LLC
Chambersburg PA
CBHW071447080526
44587CB00014B/2022